# UNDERSEA ARCHAEOLOGY

# CHRISTOPHER LAMPTON

# UNDERSEA ARCHAEOLOGY

*Franklin Watts*
*New York/London/Toronto/Sydney/1988*
*A First Book*

*FRONTIS:* EXPLORING A WRECK OFF
THE BRITISH VIRGIN ISLANDS

Cover photograph by Jonathan Blair, Woodfin Camp & Associates.

Photographs courtesy of: Uniphoto Picture Agency: pp. 2 (Grogan), 29
(Stephen Thompson), 30 (Greg Brown); Museum of Natural History:
pp. 8, 11, 17 (bottom); The Bettmann Archive: p. 13; Ocean Images, Inc.:
pp. 17 (top left and right—Charles Nicklin), 24 (Al Giddings), 36 (top—
Rosemary Chastney); NOAA: p. 19; The Cousteau Society: pp. 32, 36
(bottom); Swedish Information Service: pp. 43 (Maritime Museum and the
Warship Wasa), 49 and 50 (Wasa Museum, Stockholm, Sweden); UPI/
Bettmann Newsphotos: pp. 53, 57, 58, 63; Woods Hole Oceanographic
Institution: pp. 66 (top), 66 (bottom—Rod Catanach WHOI), 69, 70 (both),
71, 73, 75 (both); AT&T Bell Laboratories: p. 79; NASA: pp. 81 (both), 83.

Library of Congress Cataloging-in-Publication Data

Lampton, Christopher.
Undersea archaeology.

(A First book)
Bibliography: p.
Includes index.
Summary: Discusses the use of new technology in
efforts to retrieve artifacts from the ocean floor,
the exploration of shipwrecks such as the Vasa,
Mary Rose, and Titanic, and the recovery of the
Challenger spacecraft.
1. Underwater archaeology—Juvenile literature.
2. Titanic (Steamship)—Juvenile literature.
3. Challenger (Spacecraft)—Accidents—Juvenile
literature. [1. Underwater archaeology.
2. Shipwrecks. 3. Archaeology] I. Title.
CC77.U5L36   1988      930.1′028′04      87-25236
ISBN 0-531-10492-3

# CONTENTS

# UNDERSEA ARCHAEOLOGY

*Ancient North American Indian household utensils carved from wood, displayed in the Museum of Natural History in New York*

# CHAPTER ONE

# HISTORY BENEATH THE SEA

The human race has been around for quite a while, at least compared to the average human lifetime. As we near the end of the twentieth century, there are fewer and fewer people who can remember what life was like before the year 1900, and it has been a long time since anybody could recall the era before the American Civil War, or the American Revolution.

The memories of individual human beings are short, so it is important that we make an extra effort to preserve the knowledge of the past, before it is gone forever. This is a task that falls to historians, whose job it is to record the events of bygone eras (often while they are still going by) for the edification of generations yet unborn.

The practice of recording history is quite old. We have documents that can be loosely described as historical from many thousands of years ago. But although such documents may tell us much about the rise and fall of kings, they often fail to tell us other things we really want to know: What was everyday life like in the past? What did people wear? How did they build their houses? What sorts of pots did they cook their meals in?

Recorded history is valuable, but more valuable still is the ability to actually touch the past, to enter a house lived in by a common, or uncommon, person of two thousand years ago, to handle a cooking pot from ancient Greece, to see a picture of the clothing worn by a Roman soldier—to possess, in short, a manufactured object, an **artifact,** of long ago.

Unfortunately, these artifacts of the past are all too often destroyed in the name of progress. Old buildings are torn down so that new ones can be built. Old pots are discarded and replaced by newer ones.

Progress has its advantages. The new buildings and pots are often better than the old ones, though not always. But the old ones, if preserved, could tell us more about the way our ancestors lived than a shelf filled with history books.

The job of discovering artifacts—manufactured objects—from the past falls to a special breed of historian-scientists called **archaeologists.** Archaeologists are trained to discover the forgotten and buried remnants of the past, usually digging them out of the very earth itself.

Alas, time and human nature often work against the archaeologist. Even when the old is not torn down to make way for the new, the erosive effects of weather wear away at buildings and objects until they are indistinguishable from the ground they once sat on. In addition, scavenging thieves steal historically valuable works of art from tombs to sell them to merchants, or tourists remove pieces of ancient shrines as souvenirs. By the time the archaeologist arrives, the remains of the past are long gone.

Sometimes, by the sheerest good luck, a large portion of the tangible past survives intact, protected for hundreds or thousands of years until an archaeologist can unearth it in one piece, as King Tut's tomb lay beneath the shifting sands of Egypt or as the city of Pompeii lay beneath the lavas of Mount Vesuvius. It is at those fortunate moments that we come closest to touching the past itself.

*The ancient statues in this temple on the Nile*
*have been badly eroded by weather.*

The near-perfect preservation of artifacts from the past is rare. Over hundreds and thousands of years there are many dire fates that can befall an artifact, and it is a rare piece of history that escapes intact. But there is one place on earth where artifacts can survive—sometimes in nearly perfect condition—for many centuries, out of the reach of weather and vandals. That place is at the bottom of the sea.

An untold number of human artifacts have, at one time or another, been carried to the depths of the ocean. Whenever a ship sinks, it carries with it a tiny microcosm of the human life of its day. Entire cities have also been lost beneath the waves, either because of the constantly shifting shoreline or—in rare instances—because of some abrupt upheaval of the earth, such as an earthquake.

Until the last century, however, this treasure trove of ancient artifacts was largely out of the reach of archaeologists. It is only in the last fifty years that it has become common for archaeologists to retrieve artifacts from beneath the ocean. But bringing up old ships and their valuable contents from the bottom of the sea is no trivial task. It requires a special expertise that ordinary archaeologists don't have. And so a new branch of archaeology has developed over the last two centuries known variously as **undersea, underwater,** or **submarine archaeology.**

*Entire cities have been buried by sudden natural disasters. The city of Pompeii is one of the most famous. This view of a partially restored Pompeii, an ancient Italian city destroyed by a massive volcanic eruption, shows the arch of Nero, looking toward the Roman Forum.*

In some senses, there is no difference between underwater archaeology and ordinary, garden-variety archaeology. Like their dry-land counterparts, undersea archaeologists must carefully retrieve valuable and often delicate artifacts, identify and catalog them with great care, and attempt to preserve them using painstaking techniques acquired through careful experimentation.

But ideally, undersea archaeologists possess talents beyond those necessary for pure archaeology. In many instances they also are professional-caliber divers, with a working knowledge of the sea and its dangers. Undersea archaeologists must be familiar with the environment of the sea, an environment for which human beings are not naturally adapted, an environment in which unprepared explorers are putting their lives very much at risk. Of course, an archaeologist can always hire divers to retrieve artifacts and then monitor the work from a nearby boat. But the best archaeology is performed when an archaeologist is at the site itself—at the shipwreck or the city beneath the waves.

There is a special romance to undersea archaeology. It is the romance of the sea, of sailing and ancient shipwrecks. There is magic in the thought that pieces of the past lie at the bottom of the ocean, waiting for someone to retrieve them from the murky depths. In this book, we will look at some of the history and traditions of undersea archaeology, and the technology that has made it possible. And we will tell the stories of some of the more interesting explorations into the history that lies beneath the sea.

# CHAPTER TWO

# THE
# NEW
# FRONTIER

It has been said, with some truth, that we know less about the bottom of the ocean than we know about the surface of the moon. And, in some ways, the bottom of the ocean is as inaccessible to human beings as the moon. A person who dives unprotected into the sea will drown after only a few minutes underwater. Even if this hapless diver could somehow remain alive and swimming long enough to reach great depths, he or she would be crushed to death by the tremendous weight of the water itself. The sea is an environment for fish, not for human beings.

But we are a species of explorers, with an eternal need to investigate new environments, whatever the difficulties and dangers. It was inevitable that human beings would find a way to enter the domain of the sea. Attempts to build underwater apparatuses go back to the Middle Ages, but the systematic exploration of sunken ships for archaeological purposes only began in the first half of the nineteenth century.

According to historian Alexander McKee, himself an undersea archaeologist of renown (see Chapter Five), the first person to use a mechanical diving apparatus for archaeological purposes was John

Deane, who invented his own diving equipment in England in the 1820s. The invention, by at least one account, was accidental. Deane was helping a local farmer put out a fire in a stable. The horses in the stable, panicked by the fire, refused to leave, and Deane decided to go in and lead them out. The smoke, however, was too thick, and so Deane removed the helmet from an old suit of armor, ran an air pump inside it, and placed it over his head. With the helmet in place, he plunged into the smoke and saved the horses.

Not one to let a good idea go to waste, Deane soon began using the helmet and pump arrangement for undersea exploration. He added lead weights to his shoes to keep himself from floating—and turning upside down—in the water. By placing the pump on board a boat, Deane was able to explore a small wreck off the English coast and bring up artifacts such as anchors from it.

This was the start of an illustrious career. Deane spent the rest of his life in the systematic exploration and salvaging of sunken ships. Although many of these were fairly recent wrecks, which were more appealing for the monetary value of the salvaged equipment than for historical reasons, some were of genuine archaeological interest.

As McKee tells it, Deane was a true archaeologist, at least in spirit. He used watercolor artists to render likenesses of the most important artifacts retrieved from the sea, just as a modern archaeologist would take photographs of a find. He even published these pictures and relevant notes.

Among the historically significant shipwrecks explored by Deane were the *Royal George* and the *Mary Rose*. We will have more to say about the *Mary Rose* in a later chapter.

Deane was not the first person to use a mechanical device to explore the sea bottom, but his diving apparatus was lighter and more convenient than the clumsy **diving bells** in favor at the time and required far fewer people to operate. (For more about these early diving bells, see Chapter Four.) Others made improvements to Deane's basic diving apparatus in the mid-nineteenth century, particularly Augustus Siebe.

Above left:
*early divers used bells like this one, called the Sturmius bell, to salvage wrecks. They breathed air trapped inside the bell.*
Above right: *an early diving suit.*
Below: *the bathysphere was an early diving bell developed by William Beebe for undersea exploration.*

In time, it became obvious that diving was not without its perils, in addition to the obvious one of inadvertent drowning. Perhaps the greatest of these perils was—and still is—the condition known as the **bends,** which strikes divers who spend too much time at too great a depth and then resurface too quickly. The symptoms include extremely painful cramps, leading in many cases to paralysis or death. The bends are caused by a buildup of nitrogen in the bloodstream when breathing highly pressurized air. The nitrogen forms deadly bubbles when the diver returns to breathing unpressurized air on the surface. These bubbles cause extreme pain when they lodge in the blood vessels in the diver's joints. The bends can be prevented by making frequent "decompression stops" on the way back to the surface. Sometimes a diver with the bends can be cured by being placed in a so-called **recompression chamber,** which simulates the pressures found deep under the water. But the causes and cures of the bends were not recognized until the twentieth century.

John Deane's exploits demonstrated that undersea archaeology was alive and well in the nineteenth century. But the date that is often given as the beginning of the field was the dawn of the next century: 1900. It was in that year that one of the most famous and exciting of all undersea discoveries was made—the Antikythera wreck.

* * * *

Every country has its cash crop, whether that crop is tobacco or potatoes or squash or whatever. Cash crops are planted and raised by farmers who harvest them when they are ripe and take them to market and sell them for money.

But there is a crop that grows wild at the bottom of certain seas, waiting for someone intrepid enough to dive into the water and harvest it. It is not a plant, as tobacco and potatoes are, but an animal. It is called a sponge, and it thrives in such areas as the Mediterranean, the vast inland sea bordered on the north by Europe and on the south by Africa. In such countries as Greece, a

*a recompression chamber*

long tradition of sponge diving—the harvesting of the sponge crop—has been practiced by generations of sponge divers.

The earliest Greek sponge divers used only their own strength and the power of their lungs to protect them from the perils of the deep. By the late nineteenth century, however, the sponge divers had adopted the new diving technology that allowed such men as John Deane to explore wrecks on the sea bottom. Dressed in diving gear and helmets, the sponge divers could walk around on the floor of the Mediterranean and its adjoining seas and inlets, plucking the sponges from their sea-bottom homes.

The Mediterranean is a region rich in history, and some of that history took place at sea. Perhaps it was inevitable that the sponge divers would eventually stumble into something other than sponges.

In the year 1900, Captain Dimitrios Kondos was sailing home from a sponge-diving expedition when his boat was caught in a storm. He took refuge in a sheltered and deserted harbor on the island of Antikythera and waited there with his crew until the storm ended. While they waited, Kondos and his divers decided to search the waters of the harbor for sponges.

The first diver to descend was a Greek named Elias Stadiatis. Stadiatis put on a heavy diving outfit consisting of a canvas suit and metal helmet and stepped off the boat into the waters of the harbor. His only supply of oxygen came from a rubber hose connected to an air pump aboard ship. The dive was a deep one; Stadiatis descended more than 150 feet (45 m) before he reached bottom.

Suddenly, to the surprise of those waiting on the boat above, Stadiatis began ascending, climbing rapidly through the depths back to the safety of the boat. In a wild panic, he clambered onto the ship, babbling incoherently about the bodies of men, women, and horses at the bottom of the harbor. According to some accounts, Stadiatis carried with him the disembodied arm of a man—but it was fashioned from metal!

Whether or not he had managed to carry such evidence to the surface with him, Stadiatis' story was doubted by others aboard the ship. Still in a state of panic, Stadiatis was in no condition to dive again. Instead, Captain Kondos donned the diver's outfit and plunged into the harbor. And when he reached the bottom, he found almost exactly what Stadiatis had described—except that these were definitely not the bodies of once-living human beings but statues half-buried in the muck. Kondos returned to the surface with word of his discovery. (According to at least one account of the story, it was Kondos rather than Stadiatis who brought the arm back with him, which makes sense, given Stadiatis' panicky state.)

Kondos understood the meaning of this discovery. If the statues had been left behind by some ancient Greek shipwreck—as seemed likely—then they would have great value. They might not only be historic relics but fabulous works of art, for which collectors would be willing to pay dearly. But they were also a portion of Greek history and as such were the domain of the archaeologist, not the art dealer.

There is some controversy over what happened next. As the story is usually told—indeed, as it was published in an archaeological journal of the period—Kondos returned to his home on the island of Syme and told others of his find. A debate arose over what should be done with these historic works of art. Sell them to merchants and retire on the funds, counseled Kondos' greedier friends. But others pointed out that Kondos had a responsibility to his Greek ancestors to see that these historic relics found their way into museums, where Athenian scholars could study them.

According to this version of the story, Kondos did his duty and alerted the authorities in Athens to the wreck, without personally profiting from the treasures he had found. But there is another version of the story, told by noted undersea archaeologist Peter Throckmorton in his book *Shipwrecks and Archaeology: The Unharvested Sea*. According to Throckmorton, there are persistent rumors, and some evidence, that Kondos "mined" the wreck (as Throckmorton puts it) for small bronze works of art before returning to Syme, then sold these pieces to merchants over a period of years, for personal profit.[1] At this late date, however, there is probably no way to learn whether or not this version of the story is true.

Whatever the truth of the matter, Kondos and Stadiatis, the diver who had initially discovered the statues, eventually found themselves in Athens, bringing word of the treasure of Antikythera to the authorities. They arrived at an important moment in Greek archaeological history. Greece, and Athens in particular, was an important center of ancient civilization; it was, and is, a land filled with archaeological treasures. Hence, it was also a favorite gathering place for archaeologists from all over the world, who dug up ancient treasures from the Greek soil—and all too often carried them away to other countries to be studied and exhibited. To the archaeologists, of course, Greece represented a cornucopia of valuable artifacts. To the Greeks, the archaeologists must have seemed like scholarly pirates come to plunder their national treasures.

By 1900 the Greeks had raised their own crop of young archaeologists and were ready to take charge of their own history, to dig up artifacts that would be studied by Greeks and that would be exhibited in Greek museums. And what better place to begin the Greek study of Greece than with the statues at Antikythera?

An expedition was formed, financed by the Greek government. Kondos and his divers, in exchange for a handsome reward, agreed to return to Antikythera and, with the aid of a specially equipped ship, raise the statues from the bottom of the harbor.

The first dive took place on a windy, stormy day. The diver returned from the bottom carrying a statue of a bearded man, which soon came to be known as the Philosopher of Antikythera. Other divers swiftly returned with similar finds: old clay jugs, swords, pieces of marble from other statues.

Alas, the time that these artifacts had spent underwater had taken its toll. They were eaten away, eroded. Work continued, but for many days these eroded fragments were all that the divers could unearth from the harbor. In time, however, the divers managed to piece together a bronze statue that had not been eroded by the sea. The statue, when reassembled, turned out to be the work of a master sculptor named Lycippus, from the fourth century.

Although Lycippus had been known by historians for many years, this was the only one of his works to survive into the twentieth century. It was a major find indeed! Extra ships were sent to aid in the exhumation of the old wreck.

Many more works of art were found on board the ship. However, the most amazing thing salvaged from the ancient wreck was not a work of art at all but a kind of ancient computer! This device, which came to be called the Astrolabium, was made of bronze and contained wheels and gears. At first it was believed that only a portion of the device had been salvaged from the wreck, making it impossible to figure out what purpose it might have had. But ultimately, scientists determined that it was, in fact, a complete and nearly operational working model of the solar system—scaled down considerably, of course!

The Astrolabium consisted of three dials, which could be turned independently. The outer dial represented the fixed constellations of the zodiac. The inner dials, which no longer were in complete working order, represented the moon, sun, and planets. The Astrolabium worked as a kind of combination planetarium/calendar. Astronomers—or ships' navigators, who found their way around by the stars—could use the device to compute the positions of the heavenly bodies on any given night.

The salvaging of the ancient wreck took nine months, many of which fell during the stormy Mediterranean winter. According to Throckmorton, it was "the deepest salvage job in the history of diving up to that time."[2] One diver died of the bends during the grueling effort.

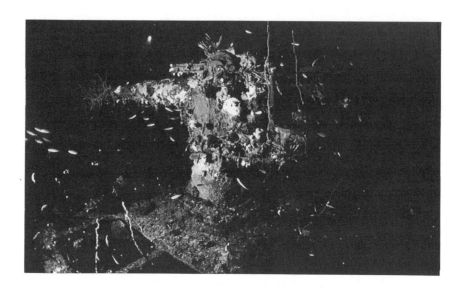

*Coral and sponge cling to a sunken bow gun from an ancient wreck. A diver can be seen, searchlight in hand, very faintly in the upper left center of the picture. Sponge divers from the past were almost the only ones likely to discover such wrecks.*

The treasure in the wreck, however, was fabulous indeed. Ultimately, enough works of art were retrieved to fill an entire gallery at the Athens National Museum.

Where had this mysterious wreck come from? Why was this treasure trove of art masterpieces lying at the bottom of a cove on the island of Antikythera? The Astrolabium seemed to indicate that the ship had sunk in the year 80 B.C., apparently while on its way from Greece to Rome. Perhaps it was carrying ransacked art treasures to Rome, most likely to the dictator Lucius Cornelius Sulla. Or, it might have been a pirate ship that stole such treasures wherever it came to land. Whatever the case, it must have encountered a storm much like the one that had originally driven Captain

Kondos into the cove at Antikythera. But the crew of the ancient ship was not as lucky as Kondos had been. Their ship had foundered and the art treasures had been lost . . . until the twentieth century.

* * * *

In 1907, another team of sponge divers was exploring the seabed off Mahdia, in Tunisia. One of the divers uncovered some oddly shaped objects in the mud. He thought they were cannon. He resurfaced and described what he had seen. Doubting the story, several more divers were sent down. The "cannon" turned out to be ancient Greek columns, encrusted with undersea organisms. Among the columns were a number of small antique objects, including bowls, candelabras, and statuettes. The divers gathered all the objects they could find and returned to the surface. In short order the antiques were all sold to merchants in Tunis for a tidy profit.

Not long after, a French archaeologist named Alfred Merlin stumbled upon one of these merchants at a street bazaar. He immediately recognized the objects that the merchant was selling as ancient Greek works of art and inquired as to their source. The merchant was reluctant to tell him, but somehow Merlin managed to loosen the man's tongue, perhaps with an offer of cash, and learned that the antiques had been found by divers.

Excited, Merlin quickly contacted the divers who had discovered the objects. When told of the mysterious Greek columns in the mud, Merlin realized that they were probably the remains of a ship that had sunk near Mahdia thousands of years earlier. Contacting other scholars and officials, Merlin hastily organized an expedition to the site and took the sponge divers along.

But the divers could no longer remember exactly where the site was. For eight days Merlin and his crew wandered along the coast of Mahdia in a boat, with divers intermittently going to the bottom to look for the lost ship. Finally it was found, and the search for new antiquities among the buried columns began.

At first nothing turned up. On their previous trip the divers had taken all of the objects that they could find, and there appeared to be nothing left. But eventually the ancient ship itself was discovered under the mud, and within it the divers found riches far beyond anything they had discovered on their first expedition.

The ship was a treasure trove of old sculptures, just as the Antikythera ship had proved to be a few years earlier. Statues of gods in the style of the Greek sculptors Lycippus and Praxiteles were brought to the surface. In addition, the ship contained the kinds of ordinary objects, such as lamps and cooking pots, that tell archaeologists so much about the way everyday life was lived in ancient times.

The excavation of the ship turned out to be quite a dangerous affair. The ship lay deep beneath the water, and the divers knew nothing of modern methods (only then being developed elsewhere in the world) of avoiding the bends. Many divers on the expedition were crippled for life by this malady.

The salvage effort took six long summers. The recovered artifacts were transported to the El Alaoui Museum in Tunis.

Where had this particular ancient ship come from? One theory was that, like the ship at Antikythera, it had been a Roman ship returning from Greece with a load of plundered works of art, probably at the direction of the dictator Sulla. But Alfred Merlin, the archaeologist in charge of the Mahdia expedition, had another theory. He said there were indications that the works of art uncovered in the Mahdia wreck were not original Greek works but copies from a later (though still ancient) century. Perhaps such works had been produced by artists in Greece, to be transported by ship to Rome, where they would be purchased by wealthy men. Such a ship might have been blown off course and foundered on the coast of Africa, only to be uncovered by twentieth-century sponge divers.

# CHAPTER THREE

# COUSTEAU

After the Mahdia expedition, underwater archaeology languished. Over the next few decades there were only a few expeditions of note, none of them as major as the two that had opened the century.

One spectacular exception to the lack of underwater archaeology in the first half of this century occurred in the early 1930s, when the Italian dictator, Benito Mussolini, ordered an entire lake drained so that two ancient Roman ships could be recovered. Pumps were set up, the water was removed, and the two sunken ships appeared, though they were later destroyed during World War II. Needless to say, this is the kind of expensive operation that most undersea archaeologists cannot afford.

Perhaps undersea archaeology was too expensive—and too difficult. The diving gear of the first half of the twentieth century was cumbersome and not well adapted to strenuous underwater work. Divers must have felt as though they were trapped in suits of armor. (How ironic that John Deane's original diving helmet actually was part of a suit of armor!)

Beginning in the 1930s, a series of inventions lightened the diver's load, ultimately making undersea archaeology a feasible occupation. The first of these were **diving flippers**. Worn on the feet, these web-footed contraptions allowed the diver to move forward through the water very rapidly. Although the flippers did not increase the amount of time that divers could remain submerged without air, they did allow them to take maximum advantage of that time.

The **diving mask**, a glass-plated device strapped to the diver's face, cleared the diver's vision, making it easier to see what lay beneath the waves. The **snorkel**, a rubber tube that extends into the air above the diver's head and feeds in air while the diver faces downward into the water, allowed the diver to spend more time examining the ocean bottom and less time coming up for air.

But the invention that really opened the sea for human exploration was the **scuba**, or *s*elf-*c*ontained *u*nderwater *b*reathing *a*pparatus.

\* \* \* \*

The co-inventor, and first user, of the scuba is almost certainly the most famous diver of modern times: Jacques Yves Cousteau. In the early 1940s Cousteau, already an accomplished diver, was looking for some sort of device that would allow him to remain underwater for long periods of time in a relatively unencumbered state. He detested the traditional diving gear but could find nothing to serve in its stead.

One device that he experimented with was a simple rubber tube that carried oxygen from a pump on land (or in a boat) to a mask worn by the diver below. But the tube had a tendency to come loose from the pump, and divers breathing the pressureless air remaining in the tube could do severe damage to their lungs.

Another device was the oxygen rebreather, which recirculated the diver's own exhalations, passing them through a filter and then mixing them with pure oxygen. But on Cousteau's first attempt to dive with the rebreather, the pure oxygen caused his body to go

*Scuba diving gear includes a mask,*
*a snorkel, flippers, and air tanks.*

into convulsions when he reached a certain depth. So much for the rebreather.

Finally, Cousteau took his problem to an engineer named Emile Gagnan, who was developing a special valve to allow automobiles to run on cooking gas. (This was during World War II, when gasoline was strictly rationed.) Gagnan adapted the valve for breathing oxygen and—*Voila!*—the scuba was born!

\* \* \* \*

The most important feature of the scuba is the "demand" valve. When the diver breathes in, the valve delivers air; when the diver stops breathing, the air stops. When the diver breathes out, the exhaled air is vented harmlessly into the water. The valve is attached to one or more tanks of compressed air. Air is held in these tanks at about 150 times the pressure of normal air at sea level. This allows about an hour's air supply to be squeezed into a single tank. As the diver plunges deeper into the water, the pressure

*Unlike fish, humans must bring their air with them when they dive into the water. The most significant feature of the scuba is the "demand valve," which lets humans breathe naturally underwater.*

of the air fed through the valve is automatically increased to match the pressure of the water surrounding the diver, which helps the diver's body to withstand the water pressure.

Scuba gear is light and not very cumbersome, thus freeing the diver to move about as he or she would on the surface. In fact, the diver is actually a great deal more free underwater than on the surface, because the buoyancy of the water and the light weight of the diving apparatus permit a kind of movement that would be impossible in air. The diver may move vertically—up and down—as well as horizontally, allowing a form of "flight" not unlike the way birds fly through the air.

Although scuba gave the diver a new kind of freedom, it did not remove the perils of the deep. In some ways, it increased them.

For instance, although the bends were no more severe with scuba than with the older diving gear, they were no less severe either. A diver with the ability to move freely in the vertical dimension might be tempted to resurface too quickly, without bothering to take the time necessary for the body to rid itself of excess nitrogen.

And a brand new peril was revealed when Cousteau and his friends began using scuba: **nitrogen narcosis**, or rapture of the depths. Although this is not the same condition as the bends, like the bends it is caused by a buildup of nitrogen in the bloodstream at great depths. The effect on the diver is one of drunkenness, a giddy sense of well-being. In this state, the diver may forget that he or she is far below the surface of the ocean and incapable of breathing water. Some divers have been known to whip off their breathing hoses under the influence of nitrogen narcosis—and summarily drown.

\* \* \* \*

Cousteau made his first dive using scuba gear in June 1943, in a secluded cove on the French Riviera. World War II was raging and France was an occupied nation, but Cousteau glided for long min-

utes underwater as though he had no troubles in the world. He plucked lobsters from the roof of an underwater cove, then surfaced and handed them to his startled wife. He described this historic first dive in his book *The Silent World:*

> *I swam across the rocks and compared myself favorably with the sars [fish]. . . . I thought of the helmet diver arriving where I was on his ponderous boots and struggling to walk a few yards, obsessed with his umbilici and his head imprisoned in copper. . . . From this day forward we would swim across miles of country no man had known, free and level, with our flesh feeling what the fish scales know.[3]*

A new age of diving had begun, and a new age of underwater archaeology, a field in which Cousteau was soon to be at the forefront.

* * * *

Cousteau shared his diving apparatus with his diving friends, including Frederic Dumas and Philippe Tailliez. These men and others were soon engaged in a number of underwater projects, some of which involved historic ships.

One of the first such ships visited by Cousteau was the Mahdia wreck, first brought to public attention in 1907 by Alfred Merlin (see Chapter Two). Cousteau was familiar with the famous wreck and in fact had talked about it with the aging Merlin himself. In 1948, with a map of the site in hand, Cousteau and his crew sailed for Mahdia.

But when they arrived at the site, they could not find the wreck. The landmarks noted on the old map had changed in the intervening forty-one years.

*Jacques Yves Cousteau*

Cousteau ordered the crew to begin standard search procedures, crisscrossing the bottom of the ocean searching for the lost Roman ship. They did not find it. The divers widened their area of search, moving closer to the shore. Still no luck. Then, on the sixth day of searching, one of the divers splashed out of the water to announce that he had found an old column buried in mud at the bottom of the sea. Indeed, this was the first evidence the sponge divers in 1907 had had of the ship! It must be the Mahdia wreck! After an evening of celebration, Cousteau and his divers began their exploration.

The Cousteau expedition was quite different from the expedition of 1907. Now the divers had scuba gear and were free to maneuver about in the underwater ruins. It was immediately clear that the buried wreck was a large ship indeed.

More artifacts were raised, and Cousteau's crew brought some of the columns back to the ship as well. They explored portions of the ship itself, learning much about how the ancient Romans built their seagoing vessels.

It was an auspicious start to Cousteau's career in undersea archaeology and to the undersea archaeology of the mid-twentieth century. But Cousteau's greatest contribution to the field—indeed, the contribution that made undersea archaeology into a major branch of historical science—took place five years later, in 1953, on the island of Grand Congloue.

\* \* \* \*

The diver's name was Christianini. He had worked the sea bottom around Marseilles for many years, mostly selling the lobsters that he found. Like many divers he eventually succumbed to a case of the bends and was rushed to a hospital where a special recompression chamber was used to ease the nitrogen bubbles from his blood. But he arrived at the hospital too late, and his toes had to be amputated, ending his career as a professional diver.

While in the hospital, Christianini met with Cousteau's friend Frederic Dumas and told him where a large number of lobsters could be found in the waters off a deserted island called Grand Congloue. Dumas had little interest in the old man's secret cache of lobsters but grew considerably more interested when Christianini mentioned that the area around the lobster bed was littered with old clay jars.

Dumas recognized immediately that the "old clay jars" must be **amphorae**, vase-like containers used for storage by the ancient Greeks. Since materials to be transported by ship were often placed in amphorae by the Greeks, the presence of many amphorae beneath the water must indicate the presence of a sunken ship. Dumas noted the location where the old man had seen the amphorae and transmitted the news to Cousteau.

Cousteau and his crew, aboard their famous boat *Calypso,* set sail for Grand Congloue, to look for the remains of a Greek ship. Also on board was an archaeologist named Fernand Benoit, an expert on ancient artifacts. Cousteau and his crew didn't know it yet, but they were about to discover what would be the oldest sunken ship known up to that time!

When the *Calypso* arrived at Grand Congloue, Dumas dived into the water and spent twenty minutes searching for the wreck. He did not find it. He returned to the ship with the bad news.

Discouraged, Cousteau decided to make a dive before they gave up the search. The sea bottom off Grand Congloue turned out to be fairly deep—about 170 feet (51 m)—and Cousteau began to develop a mild case of nitrogen narcosis. Just as he was ready to resurface, he saw the neck of an old jar sticking out of the muck. An amphora! And behind the amphora was a great mound of sea floor that obviously concealed the hulk of an old ship—a very *large* old ship!

Cousteau spent a few moments decompressing in shallow water, then bobbed to the surface with the good news. He had found the wreck!

A team of divers was immediately organized, and they began to pick away at the mounds of rubble that lay atop the ancient ship. However, some of the rocks that needed to be moved were huge, so

a ship with a winch was recruited for the task. Eventually, all but one of the rocks—a 30-ton monster—were removed, and the more delicate part of excavating the wreck began.

A good many fragments of ancient artifacts were discovered as the site was cleared off, but it soon became obvious that the truly valuable artifacts would be harder to reach. By this time the cold winter wind called the mistral was blowing. As icy winds whipped the waves into a froth, the work became very uncomfortable both for those in the water and those on board the ship.

Dozens of amphorae were raised from the sea in the following weeks. Raising the delicate old jars without breaking them was a particularly thorny problem. One method that worked well with unbroken amphorae was to use a pump to fill the amphora with air, then let the jar rise to the surface under its own buoyant power, where it would leap out of the water like a flying fish!

The next stage of excavation involved use of a suction pump, which the crew nicknamed the "underwater vacuum cleaner" or "mud sucker." The pump, a wide pipe attached to a powerful air pump aboard ship, could suck water, dirt, and even artifacts right off the bottom of the sea. Back on the boat, the materials pumped up were filtered through a mesh basket, so that no artifacts could escape back into the sea.

A diver would hold one end of the pump at the undersea site, clearing away debris like a sculptor chipping away stone from a statue. All manner of items would find their way into the pump— and eventually into the basket on the boat. The occasional squid or

Above: *from Havana Harbor, Cuba, a diver retrieves an amphora once used for storing olive oil.* Below: *Cousteau's ship, the* Calypso.

lobster that ended up in this contraption would be tossed into a second basket, for later consumption at the dinner table!

However, the powerful pump also had a tendency to destroy delicate artifacts, and so it had to be used with care. Slowly the mound of dirt that covered the ship was pumped away, revealing the outline of the ancient wreck beneath.

Literally thousands of amphorae were raised from the wreck. Some of them were filled with a peculiar assortment of pebbles and shells. The divers discovered that each of these amphorae also contained a squid hiding among the shells.

But what did the amphorae originally contain? An unbroken amphora was recovered with its seal still intact, and it was opened. Inside was . . . wine! The amphora had been used for shipping wine!

Unable to resist the temptation to sample wine that had been aged for 2,200 years, Cousteau swallowed a mouthful. "I tasted the mustiness of the ages in that wraithy wine," he later wrote in his book *The Living Sea.* The alcohol had evaporated from the wine centuries before. Seeing the look on Cousteau's face, a shipmate joked, "Bad vintage century?"[4]

Alas, this was the only one of the thousands of amphorae that still contained wine. How valuable it would have been if scientists could have studied the chemical composition of that ancient wine.

Interestingly, there were other amphorae that were still intact, but the wine had apparently been drained through carefully drilled holes, indicating that the sailors had been tippling from the wine that comprised their cargo. This led to speculation that the ship had gone down not in a storm but because of the drunkenness of its crew.

The deeper the divers dug into the wreck, the more intact were the artifacts they found. Consider, for instance, the bowls. At first they found fragments of bowls, then they found fragments of bowls with hints of black pigment still on them, indicating that the bowls were once painted. Finally, intact bowls still painted black were unearthed. (Shortly before the intact bowls were discovered, one diver painted a bowl black with shoe polish, as a practical joke on one of the archaeologists.) After a large number of bowls were recovered, the crew of the *Calypso* held a banquet, actually using these ancient bowls. To the surprise of many of those present, the black bowls did their job as well or better than their modern counterparts—and were also a great deal more attractive, largely because their black coloration set off the colors of the food quite vividly.

* * * *

Cousteau had originally intended that the *Calypso* remain at the Grand Congloue site for two months. But two months passed and the work was barely begun. It was decided that the *Calypso* would leave, but that a base camp would be established on Grand Congloue Island itself. The camp was given the unofficial name of Port Calypso.

The mistral continued, growing more severe in midfall, but the divers persisted in their efforts to salvage the old wreck. New divers were hired. One day, a diver named Serventi was given the job of freeing a trapped anchor at the bottom of the sea.

Serventi went down but did not return. Worried, Cousteau sent a second diver, named Falco, to look for him. Falco found Serventi lying on the bottom, unconscious. Serventi was rushed to a hospital, where he was put into a recompression chamber. But he was dead and could not be revived.

This was a turning point for Cousteau. He had never had to deal with the death of one of his divers before, and he began to question whether the excavation of an old wreck was worth a human life. It was not, he decided. As he wrote in *The Living Sea:* "Did I have the right to risk lives to bring up old jars? The unarguable answer was, *No.*"[5]

Yet even as he came to this conclusion, a message arrived from another diver begging to take Serventi's place so that the work could go on. Moved by this testimony to the importance of his excavation, Cousteau decided that Serventi would have wished for him to continue. The excavation of the Grand Congloue wreck went on.

In fact, it went on for some time, but Cousteau was never able to raise the entire ship, although that had been his original desire.

* * * *

The question of where the Grand Congloue ship came from—that is, how it ended up at the bottom of the sea—was a tantalizing one and was pursued at some length by Professor Benoit.

Benoit noticed that many of the artifacts—amphorae, dishes, and so on—raised from the wreck were marked with the letters SES. He guessed that these were the first letters of someone's name, since this was a common Greek method of abbreviation.

Through extensive research, Benoit found out that there had been a wealthy Roman family named Sestius, which might have been abbreviated SES. And one member of this family, Marcus Sestius, had been a shipowner. Could he have shipped out the cargo that found its way into the sea off Grand Congloue?

Cousteau's crew paid a visit to the island of Delos, where Sestius had lived, to find out. There they visited the ruins of old houses, from the time of the ancient Greeks. And, sure enough, one of these houses contained the letters SES marked on its floors. Not only did these mosaics contain the crucial abbreviation, they also depicted a trident symbol that had been present on many of the jars raised from the bottom of the sea.

So the ship had almost certainly belonged to Marcus Sestius, of the second century B.C. There were even indications, but no proof, that the loss of the ship may have financially ruined Sestius, all those many centuries ago.

# CHAPTER FOUR

# THE
# VASA

The raising of the Swedish warship *Vasa* is one of the most spectacular successes in all of underwater archaeology. It is the story of how one man began a campaign to raise a three-hundred-year-old piece of Swedish history from the watery grave in which it had lain for centuries.

That, of course, is the twentieth century portion of the story. But the true beginning of the story of the *Vasa* lies deep in the past. . . .

* * * *

It was the year 1625. The Thirty-Years' War (1618–1648) was raging in Europe. King Gustavus II of Sweden feared that the war would soon arrive on his doorstep, putting his country at the mercy of the Holy Roman Empire, which was then subjugating so many European nations.

The Swedish king decided to build a powerful navy to defend Sweden and its allies. For the flagship of that navy he would build the most powerful and magnificent warship ever!

To accomplish this, he summoned the master shipbuilder, Henrik Hybertsson, and asked him to design and build four warships, one of which was to be the magnificent flagship, the *Vasa*.

It took three years for the *Vasa* to be built and readied for its maiden voyage. During that time Hybertsson died, but the ship was completed without him, according to his plans. And it was magnificent indeed, decked out with beautiful carvings and statues and armed with sixty-four bronze cannon in gunports that lined the sides of the ship. The *Vasa* was large as well, at least in comparison to most other ships of its time. It weighed 1,400 tons, was 150 feet (45 m) long, and 180 feet (54 m) tall, including sails—the height of an eighteen-story building. Of course, much of this height was underwater.

The maiden voyage of the *Vasa,* a symbolic voyage only, was scheduled for August 1628, and an enthusiastic crowd turned out for the occasion. King Gustavus himself watched from the nearby royal castle. It was to be his moment of triumph.

Then disaster struck. The *Vasa* set sail, fired off its cannon in salute, and was struck by a sudden gust of wind. The ship tilted wildly to one side, tossing its passengers about on the deck and nearly dumping the entire ship into the water. In desperation, the crew attempted to cut down the sails, but the ship continued to lean. The chief ordnance officer tried to move the cannon around on the lower decks to correct the *Vasa*'s balance, but his efforts came to nothing. The ship rolled again and water flowed in through the open gunports. Within moments the *Vasa* had sunk.

Most of the crew and passengers were flung into the water, where they were picked up by rescue boats. But fifty people were trapped belowdecks and went down with the *Vasa*. Fortunately, the ship was not carrying a full complement of soldiers, because the launching was a ceremonial occasion. Unfortunately, for that same reason, it was carrying women and children, and some of them died.

The captain and many of his officers were saved, but they may

*the* Vasa

have wished they had gone down with their ship. They were arrested and court-martialed almost immediately.

What followed was reminiscent in some ways of the inquest following the explosion of the space shuttle *Challenger*, a ship of a far different kind in quite another time. The court was interested in fixing blame, and so it interrogated everyone responsible for the design and building of the *Vasa*, except for two individuals: its designer, Henrik Hybertsson, who had died a year earlier, and the king.

Ultimately, the court blamed no one for the disaster, perhaps because the most likely scapegoat, Hybertsson, was dead. Also, much of the testimony implicated the king himself, since he had approved the design and urged that the ship be completed.

The court did, however, find that there had been considerable advance warning that something was wrong with the *Vasa*. Admiral Klaus Fleming, in order to determine the stability of the ship, had ordered a group of thirty men to run en masse from one side of the ship to the other. After three tries the ship was wobbling so badly that Fleming had stopped the test lest the *Vasa* capsize. Yet despite this strong evidence of the ship's unreliability, nothing had been done.

Although the court was not able to determine where the blame lay, or what precisely caused the disaster, modern experts believe that the *Vasa*'s center of gravity was too high—that is, it rode too high in the water because of insufficient ballast (stabilizing weights) to hold it lower in the water. The lack of ballast was intentional, probably designed to prevent water from flowing into the lowest gunports. Hence, the design was also at fault.

Whatever the technical reason, as of 1628 the magnificent *Vasa* lay at the bottom of the Baltic Sea. . . .

＊ ＊ ＊ ＊

The idea of raising the *Vasa*, or at least salvaging some of its valuable contents, arose almost immediately. An English engineer named Ian Bulmer offered to raise the ship only days after its sinking. Using divers to attach ropes to the *Vasa*'s masts, Bulmer attempted to pull the ship out of the water with a team of horses. He did not succeed, but he did pull the *Vasa* into an upright position, in which it remained until the twentieth century.

A few months later, the Swedish navy lowered chains and hooked ropes to the *Vasa*, anchoring them to the cannon ports. Alas, when they attempted to raise the ship, they only managed to pull loose a few pieces of it.

In the years that followed, teams of salvage experts from many countries tried to raise the *Vasa*, succeeding only in ripping its decks apart. One of the most spectacular salvage efforts was in 1664, when Albrekt von Treileben used an early diving bell to send workers down to the ship to retrieve the warship's valuable bronze cannon.

A diving bell, in this early incarnation, was simply a bell-shaped copper device that could be lowered into the water with a diver and a supply of trapped air inside. What keeps the air inside the bell? You can discover this for yourself by turning an empty glass upside down and pushing it down into a sink full of water. The air will stay inside the glass until you turn it right side up. Why? Because the air, being lighter than the water, will try to rise but will be blocked by the bottom of the glass—as long as the glass remains upside down.

This was the principle behind von Treileben's diving bell, which allowed divers to remain underwater for as long as thirty minutes at a time. Using this device, the divers raised fifty cannon from the *Vasa*.

After the cannon were gone, interest in salvaging the *Vasa* waned, and its location was forgotten. It might still lie beneath the Baltic Sea today if it were not for the efforts of an enthusiastic amateur undersea archaeologist.

\* \* \* \*

Anders Franzen was fascinated with the notion of raising old ships, and he knew that the waters around his native Sweden were full of such sunken vessels. But many of these vessels had been destroyed by an underwater worm called the **teredo,** or shipworm. These underwater pests eat away at the wood of old ships until nothing is left. Franzen despaired of ever finding a genuinely old ship in well-preserved condition.

In the late 1930s, he made a fortuitous discovery. Shipworms thrived only in salty water. But the Baltic Sea, which lay to the east of Sweden, had a very low salt content. There would be no shipworms there to destroy old ships!

Franzen, therefore, turned his attention to the Baltic. By studying old records, he learned of fifty ships that had gone down there near Sweden. He narrowed down this list to twelve ships and took it to the experts at the Marine Historical Museum, who recommended that he study the possibility of raising a ship called the *Riksapplet* that had been lost in 1676. But when he located this ship, he found that it had long ago been destroyed by the surf or salvaged by earlier searchers.

Next, he spoke to an historian named Nils Ahnlund, who told him that the *Vasa* would have the greatest historical value of any of the wrecks on his list. So, in 1953, Franzen turned his attention to the *Vasa.*

Finding the old warship, however, was easier said than done. Franzen pored over moldy records of the *Vasa*'s sinking and of previous attempts to raise it, with an eye toward locating the ship. But the information that he discovered was contradictory and inexact. All he could learn was that it lay somewhere near Stockholm.

Unable to find the information he needed, Franzen entered Stockholm harbor with a motorboat and a homemade **sonar** device (an instrument that detects the presence of underwater objects by bouncing sound waves off of them and listening for echoes). Using a cable with a hook on it, he dragged the bottom of the harbor, pulling up all kinds of junk but no evidence of the *Vasa.* Finally, after two years of this monotonous and unsuccessful searching, he went back to the records and found a letter that he had not seen before. It was from the Swedish Parliament to King Gustavus, dated August 12, 1628. It contained this crucial sentence: "But it happened that [the *Vasa*] got no further than Beckholmsudden, where she sank to the bottom with cannon and all else, and lies in eighteen fathoms."[6]

This was all Franzen needed to know. Beckholmsudden was an island in the harbor where he had been searching. Earlier, he had detected a strange underwater hump there with his sonar but had been told that the hump was only debris left over from some engineering operations performed in that spot a few years before.

Franzen returned to the site, lowered a **coring device** (a tube to bring up sample materials from sediment) into the water, and brought up a piece of oak. The oak had been blackened by the water. Franzen knew that oak must remain underwater for at least a century to blacken in this manner. Whatever was down there, it was made out of oak—and it was old!

Now he needed divers to investigate the site, but he didn't have money to hire any. Cleverly, he convinced a navy diving instructor to hold diving practice in the harbor, so that he could use the navy divers to search for the *Vasa*.

The first diver to descend reported that he could see nothing but mud. But just as he was about to resurface, he encountered a solid object in that mud.

"Wait a minute!" he reported. "I just reached out and touched something solid . . . it feels like a wall of wood! It's a big ship, all right! Now I'm climbing the wall . . . here are some square openings . . . must be gun ports."[7]

One hundred and ten feet (33 m) below the surface of Stockholm harbor, the diver began to climb the bulkheads of the *Vasa*. It was the first time a human being had touched the ship in nearly three centuries. The year was 1956.

＊＊＊＊

The next step was to raise the *Vasa* from its lodging in the mud. But how?

Franzen certainly didn't have the money for such an operation. Fortunately, the rediscovery of the *Vasa* had captured the imagination of the Swedish public, and donations began to pour in. Soon, Franzen had enough money to begin the project.

But even if the money were sufficient, what method could be used to raise such a large old ship from the bottom of the harbor? Although the *Vasa* had been spared by the shipworms, the wood was still old and might give way under the attempt to lift it.

Many imaginative suggestions were made as to how the *Vasa* might be raised. One possibility was to fill the ship with ping pong balls! The air in the balls would make the ship buoyant and it would float to the surface. Another suggestion was to fill the ship with refrigerant, which would freeze the *Vasa,* turning it into a floating iceberg.

All these ideas were rejected. The *Vasa* was too valuable a historical relic with which to experiment. In the end, it was decided that the *Vasa* would be raised by looping cables around it and lifting it to the surface. But, given the *Vasa*'s age, this was also risky and would have to be done with great caution.

Divers would have to wrap the cables around the *Vasa.* This was very dangerous work. The *Vasa* sat in several feet of mud. Using powerful hoses, the divers bored tunnels in the mud and actually swam beneath the old ship, carrying the cables with them! If the *Vasa*'s soggy timbers had given out, the ship could have collapsed on top of these divers, almost certainly dooming them. Fortunately, this did not happen, although one diver was trapped briefly when one of the mud tunnels collapsed.

An unexpected problem arose. The divers were superstitious. They believed that a spirit or ghost known as the Old Man guarded the wreck. Objects were sometimes whisked from the hands of divers, and this was blamed on the ghost, although it was more likely a trick of the water currents. Soon, the divers took to throwing a handful of coins into the water each day to appease the ghost. Although it is unlikely that any ghost was appeased by this action, it seems to have appeased the divers.

By August 1959, the *Vasa* was ready to be raised. A fleet of salvage ships arrived. Special pontoons—empty steel canisters—were floated above the old warship and filled with water, so that they floated just below the surface. The cables from the *Vasa* were tied to the pontoons. The water was then pumped out of the pontoons so that they would float on top of the water. As they rose, they pulled the *Vasa* up with them.

It worked! The ancient timbers of the *Vasa* held, and it rose out of the mud!

*On April 24, 1961, the* Vasa *broke the surface after 333 years on the bottom of the sea.*

*Mounted on a concrete pontoon inside an aluminum framework, the Vasa was moved to a museum in Stockholm. The city of Stockholm is seen in the background.*

The salvage operation proceeded slowly, however. The *Vasa* was moved a short distance into the harbor, then lowered to the bottom again, though it remained attached to the pontoons. Day by day it was moved farther inland. Then it was left on the bottom for another year and a half, as funds were raised for the final stage of the raising.

In April 1961, pontoons were attached to the sides of the *Vasa* to give it added buoyancy, and the mud and silt were pumped out of it. On April 24 the raising began. Finally, in early May, it reached the surface and was towed into dock.

A newly raised ship of the *Vasa*'s age is a delicate thing. It was necessary to spray its planks almost continually with water and a preservative solution so that it would not dry out and crumble to dust.

* * * *

The *Vasa* was a stunning archaeological find. It gave historians a wealth of information about how ships were built in the seventeenth century, a subject about which remarkably little was known, since no other ship of the period had survived.

Further, the contents of the *Vasa* provided a look at how individuals, especially sailors, had lived during that period. The *Vasa* was rich with important artifacts. The sleeping accommodations— bare wooden planks for the sailors, small bunks for the officers— were examined in detail. The eating utensils were small bowls, wooden spoons, a wooden dish, and knives. Crude medical equipment was found.

Casks were discovered that still contained food. One researcher actually tasted the butter and claimed that it still tasted like butter, although rancid butter. Casks were found still containing ale. The skeletal bodies of twelve crewmen were also found, many still wearing clothing with coins in the pockets. To allow others to view the *Vasa* and its recovered artifacts, a museum was built in Stockholm, which is still open to tourists.

# CHAPTER FIVE

# THE
# MARY
# ROSE

The story of the *Mary Rose* has many fascinating parallels with the story of the *Vasa* (see Chapter Four). But the *Mary Rose* was British, not Swedish. It sank nearly a century before the *Vasa*, and it was not raised until 1982.

Like Sweden in the next century, England was being threatened by a powerful enemy, in this case, France. Henry VIII, the British king, was worried. The British navy consisted of only 100 ships, while the attacking French fleet numbered 235 ships. But Henry felt ready for the battle.

The pride of Henry's fleet was the *Mary Rose*, named after the king's own sister. It was an old ship, but it had been rebuilt according to the latest ideas for constructing warships and was now laden—perhaps overly laden—with powerful bronze cannon (once again, like the *Vasa*) and other weapons. One of the innovations that Henry had added to the ship was to open gunports low on its side through which an extra row of cannon could extend, giving it greater firepower than the French ships.

A rope net called an antiboarding net had been spread across the deck of the *Mary Rose* to protect it from being boarded by

*the* Mary Rose

enemy sailors. Later, sailors aboard the warship would curse this net for trapping them inside the ship instead of protecting them from those outside.

On July 19, 1545, the aging Henry VIII stood at Southsea Castle in Portsmouth, England, and watched the approaching French armada. The English ships, including the *Mary Rose*, sailed out to meet it. The day was clear and beautiful, with little wind to fill the sails of the ships and propel them across the water.

Then a sudden breeze appeared. As the other ships cut through the sea, the *Mary Rose* tilted to one side, much as the *Vasa* would in the next century. What was wrong? The commander of the *Mary Rose*, Vice Admiral Sir George Carew, shouted a cryptic message to the captain of a nearby warship, "I have the sort of knaves I cannot rule!"

This was the last communication between the *Mary Rose* and any other ship. The warship tilted further to one side, allowing water to pour into the gunports and causing the ship to begin to sink. The men on the lower decks attempted to escape, but they were trapped by the antiboarding net. The king himself could see the entire horrifying incident from his castle, and the screams of the trapped men were clearly audible across the water. History records that Henry shouted, "Oh, my gentlemen, oh, my gallant men!" The wife of the *Mary Rose*'s commander, standing at his side, collapsed in a dead faint.

Rescue ships sailed to the *Mary Rose*'s side, but only 30 men were saved. Another 665 went down with the ship. It was one of the greatest disasters in English naval history.

\* \* \* \*

Why did the *Mary Rose* sink? As with the tragedy of the *Vasa*, it is difficult to explain such an event centuries after the fact, but we can make an educated guess. When the ship was refitted for battle, the *Mary Rose* was apparently equipped with a larger number of weapons than it was intended to carry. The warship probably became top-heavy, which contributed to its foundering in a sudden breeze. And the lower gunports certainly contributed to the ship's filling with water at a crucial moment. The comment by its commander about "knaves I cannot rule" seems to imply that the crew was out of control, and perhaps that was a factor as well.

What happened in the battle of Portsmouth after the *Mary Rose* went down? The French attacked the English but were soon repelled. There was no clear winner.

Although the *Mary Rose*, one of a hundred British ships in the fray, played little role in the battle itself, it was guaranteed a place in British history. And as it settled to the bottom of the channel called The Solent, just 40 feet (12 m) below the surface, it was inevitable that it would arouse the interest of future undersea archaeologists.

* * * *

The first undersea archaeologist to attempt to salvage the wreckage of the *Mary Rose* was, in fact, the first undersea archaeologist, John Deane (see Chapter Two). Over the course of four years, Deane and his brother brought up some cannon and timbers from the ship.

The next archaeologist to become seriously involved with the *Mary Rose* was Alexander McKee, who is also a historian (see Chapter Two). In the mid-1960s, McKee organized Project Solent Ships, which looked for wrecks in The Solent where the *Mary Rose* lay. It was not until the early 1970s, however, that McKee decided to concentrate exclusively on King Henry's warship. He had learned that the ship was buried largely beneath heavy silt, which would have kept its contents in a remarkable state of preservation.

In the spring of 1971, McKee's divers got their first look at the *Mary Rose*, where a portion of it had been uncovered by the storms of the previous winter. A *Mary Rose* committee was formed to supervise the site, and a few years later England's young Prince

Charles, himself a diver, became president of the *Mary Rose* Trust, which was organized to raise money for the salvaging of the ship.

The ship was gradually dug out from its bed of silt. Care had to be taken to keep the ancient frame of the ship from collapsing. It was not until 1979 that divers could get inside the ship and begin to remove artifacts from it.

Over the next three years the contents of the *Mary Rose* were brought up piece by piece. A series of 30,000 dives were made, ten of them by Prince Charles himself. When it was completely excavated, the raising of the ship itself began. Not all of the warship remained intact. Only the starboard half of the hull remained to be lifted from The Solent.

The raising took place on October 11, 1982. Cables were attached to the hull, and a huge floating crane lifted the warship free of the silt. A large audience, the prince included, watched the *Mary Rose* return to the open air. As it came out of the water, part of the device designed to lift it gave way, striking the ship and smashing a few timbers. It was a tense moment. Afterward, *Time* magazine quoted Prince Charles as having said, "I was slightly horrified, but the important thing is to be British and stay calm."[8]

Once the ship, which survived the incident largely unharmed, was raised, it needed to be sprayed continuously with water to keep it from drying out. It was then moved out of The Solent and into the Portsmouth harbor.

The raising of the *Mary Rose* cost, all told, $7 million. *Time* ranks it as "the most expensive underwater archaeological salvage operation in history."[9]

Was it worth it? Yes. In archaeological terms, it was worth at least that much. The *Mary Rose* was a treasure trove of valuable

*Prince Charles rests after*
*his dive to see the wreck*
*of the* Mary Rose.

*The hull of the* **Mary Rose** *is lowered onto a barge
after it is raised from its watery grave.*

artifacts, and they were as well preserved as had been anticipated.

Margaret Rule, McKee's partner in the raising of the *Mary Rose*, described some of the important artifacts in an article in *National Geographic* magazine. For instance, she said there were many pocket sundials, small devices that could be used to tell time by the shadow of the sun on their faces. These were so common on board the ship that Rule suggests they may have been as popular then as wristwatches are now.[10]

An entire chest of medical equipment was also found on board, containing sixty-four implements used by the barber/surgeon/dentist/doctors of the day (usually all the same person). The contents of the chest included bowls for draining blood from patients and a jar of well-preserved salve in which the doctor's finger marks were still visible.

Another implement that would seem bizarre to medical patients of our day is a wooden mallet used in "anesthetizing patients." Did the doctor strike the patient on the head before operating? Not exactly. According to modern experts, the patient would be wearing a metal helmet, which, when struck, would cause vibrations that would presumably have distracted the patient while surgery was being performed. Although modern anesthesia would doubtlessly have been preferable, we can hope for the patient's sake that the mallet had at least some small effect.

Fishing equipment was common on the ship. The seamen probably caught fish to add some variety to their diets, but they may also have fished just for fun and to help pass the time.

Speaking of the seamen's diets, the remains of food found aboard the *Mary Rose* indicate that the fare was almost sumptuous. Apparently, the well-nourished seamen—or at least their officers—dined on a wide variety of meats and vegetables, as well as fruits such as cherries and plums, and several types of nuts, with beer as the beverage of choice. Officers dined on elegant dinnerware made of pewter.

The bones of animals were also uncovered in the wreckage. The presence of rats was hardly surprising, since they are an age-old shipboard pest. A dog was present, apparently to chase the rats. The skeleton of a frog on the ship, however, has baffled archaeologists. Was it a pet? Was it used to indicate the direction to shore? (An old superstition held that frogs always knew the way to land and would instinctively swim in that direction.) Rule offers a simpler explanation: "The frog was kept alive in a barrel of water on deck simply to ensure that the water was fit to drink"[11]—rather like the traditional canary in the coal mine. Modern readers may feel that a barrel of water would be rendered unfit to drink merely by the presence of a frog in it, but those were more primitive times.

As with the *Vasa*, a museum to exhibit the *Mary Rose* artifacts is currently being built.

# CHAPTER SIX

# THE
# TITANIC

Undersea archaeology would not be possible without technology—the technology that allows human beings to work, and sometimes even live, beneath the sea. But technology cannot change the fact that humans are not adapted for life in the ocean deep. The deeper divers plunge beneath the waves, the more crushing the weight of the water that presses down on their lungs. And in some regions the water is so piercingly cold that no one can live for long at such temperatures. Diving suits and submersible vehicles—miniature submarines—can offset the pressure and cold temperatures to some extent, but there are limits. For some areas of exploration, it may be more feasible to send robots down into the ocean than human beings.

Robots? Aren't they something out of science fiction? Well, yes, but there are robots in the real world, too, and some robots have been built for exploring places where humans cannot, or should not, go. A case in point is the dramatic 1985 discovery of the long-lost wreckage of the *Titanic*, and the 1986 exploration of that wreckage, a search-and-reconnaissance mission performed largely by robots.

Nearly everyone has heard the story of the *Titanic*. This massive luxury liner—at 46,328 tons and 882.5 feet (231.5 m) long, the largest ship of its day—set sail from Southampton, England, on April 10, 1912, en route to New York City. It was the ship's maiden voyage, and the passenger list included many of the rich and famous people of the day, such as multimillionaire John Jacob Astor. The *Titanic* was billed as the "unsinkable" luxury liner, an irony that made its fate all the more poignant, and which may explain why it carried lifeboats for only 1,178 of its (approximately) 2,200 passengers and crew.

At just before midnight on April 14, as the *Titanic* plowed through North Atlantic waters, a lookout spied an iceberg ahead. He warned the bridge, where the officer in charge attempted to turn the ship from its collision course. In fact, the officer only succeeded in bringing the ship around into a broadside collision with the iceberg. So violent was the collision that even the "unsinkable" *Titanic* began to fill slowly with water.

The ship did not sink abruptly, as a damaged airplane falls from the sky. In fact, it was two-and-a-half hours before the *Titanic* finally slipped beneath the waves. In that time, one of the great dramas of the twentieth century was played out, a drama that has been reenacted in many books and several motion pictures, most definitively in the classic book and movie entitled *A Night to Remember*. The lifeboats were put in the water as quickly as possible, some of them not even completely filled, leaving roughly 1,500 people on board condemned to plunge into the frigid waters along with the ship. And though it was the families of the wealthy that were best represented on the lifeboats—their first-class accommodations were located nearest to the lifeboat davits—several of the world's richest men, including John Jacob Astor, died that evening, still dressed in white tie and tails.

Perhaps others would have been saved if help had arrived in time, but it did not. The *Titanic*'s desperate radio SOS was not detected by those in a nearby ship who could have helped, and the

*German artist Willy Stoewer's visualization
of the sinking of the* Titanic

ships that did respond arrived too late. At 2:20 in the morning, the survivors in the lifeboats watched as the stern of the great ship plunged into the ocean, followed by the remainder of its massive bulk. The screams of the dying echoed across the water.

It was the news story of the year, and no wonder. It had glamour, tragedy, poignance; survivors returned with stories of noble gestures and petty deeds; of the deaths of the great, the near-great, and the unknown. The story of the *Titanic* has never been forgotten, but the ship itself disappeared from the view of all human beings on that cold April morning in 1912, never to be seen again.

Never, that is, until 1985. . . .

\* \* \* \*

Finding the remains of the *Titanic* has been a dream of salvage experts practically since the night the ship foundered. There are several reasons for this. One is the mystical aura that surrounded the most famous and dramatic shipwreck of this century. Another is the belief that its safes and staterooms might hold considerable treasure, especially in the form of jewels and art objects. After all, many of the passengers were wealthy—some of them fabulously wealthy—and they might have brought valuable objects with them. There is reason to believe that this was not the case, but it has remained a persistent hope among those searching for sunken treasure.

But the location of the sunken *Titanic* was not known with the kind of precision necessary for salvage. Only recent advances in deep-sea sonar technology—the use of sound waves and echoes to detect large objects deep underwater, much as radar uses radio waves to detect airplanes or thunderstorms—has allowed recent searchers to zero in on the lost ship.

One of the most determined of the searchers for the *Titanic*, Texas oilman Jack Grimm (who has also financed searches for the Loch Ness monster and Bigfoot), funded *Titanic* searches in the early 1980s through the Scripps Oceanographic Institution of California. His searchers, aided by advanced undersea sonar and underwater cameras, found something they *thought* might be the *Titanic*, but in the storm-tossed northern seas, they never got close enough to make sure.

The team that finally found the *Titanic* was a joint French-American expedition. The Americans were from the Woods Hole Oceanographic Institution in Woods Hole, Massachusetts. The French were from the Institute for Research and Exploitation of the Sea (or IFREMER, the initials of the French version of the name). Aboard the U.S. Navy research ship *Knorr* and the French ship *Le Suroit*, the investigators set sail from their respective countries for the North Atlantic in the summer of 1985.

The three most important players in this expedition were an odd trio indeed: one was human and two were machines.

The human was Robert Ballard, marine geologist and director of the Deep Submergence Laboratory at Woods Hole. Ballard had considerable experience in exploring the deepest portions of the ocean. In 1974 he had joined Project FAMOUS, the *F*rench-*A*merican *M*id-*O*cean *U*ndersea *S*tudy, which had explored the underwater mountain range known as the Mid-Atlantic Ridge and the rift valley at its center. At 36,000 miles (57,600 km) in length, the ridge is the largest single geographical feature on earth, although most people are not even aware that it exists. New sea-bottom material spews out from beneath the earth's crust here, causing the ocean bottom to spread outward and pushing the continents on both sides of the Atlantic further and further apart.

To aid in his exploration of the ridge, Ballard brought along the tiny submersible vehicle *Alvin*, developed by the U.S. Navy in the mid-1960s for underwater research. Although it carried only three passengers, the *Alvin* could plunge more than ten times deeper than a conventional submarine, to a staggering depth of 13,000 feet (3,900 m)! With the aid of the *Alvin*, Ballard and his colleagues discovered bizarre organisms at the bottom of the sea that existed outside of the normal food chain of which almost all other creatures on earth are part. Instead of thriving on energy from the sun,

rendered into chemical form by plants through photosynthesis, these creatures live on the heat energy thrust up from beneath the earth's crust through underwater thermal vents.

By the time of the *Titanic* expedition in 1985, Ballard was thoroughly experienced in underwater exploration and discovery. This time he brought along some even more impressive devices as part of the search—*Angus* and *Argo*, the two other major players in this story.

*Angus*, the *a*coustically *n*avigated *g*eological *u*nderwater *s*urvey, is an unmanned underwater craft mounted with cameras, first used in the exploration of the ridge. *Angus* is capable of taking more than 3,000 pictures in a marathon underwater session.

*Argo* was a brand-new underwater craft that was on its maiden voyage. In fact, the search for the *Titanic* was in some ways intended as a test run for *Argo*. Although also unmanned, *Argo* has a built-in television camera and is mounted with dazzlingly bright strobe lights, so it can send back live pictures to those waiting on the surface. In a sense, *Argo* is a robot that can explore the bottom of the sea, providing "eyes" for those who cannot descend with it.

Together *Argo, Angus,* and Ballard would explore the ocean bottom looking for the *Titanic*.

\* \* \* \*

Finding the exact site of the *Titanic* was difficult because the ships that had rescued the original survivors had reported different loca-

Above: *Dr. Robert Ballard (arm raised) does some last-minute pre-dive checks on his exploring equipment.* Below: *The* Alvin *is lowered into the sea for its historic mission.*

tions for the ship's whereabouts. The expedition eventually settled on the most likely set of coordinates and began the search there. The French ship, *Le Suroit*, arrived first, in late June, and swept the area with a new device called a SAR, or *s*ystems *a*coustic *r*emote, a type of side-scanning sonar. The SAR was towed near the ocean bottom by the *Suroit*, where it broadcast sonar pulses and measured how far the echoes traveled, while the scientists above waited for signals that would indicate the presence of a large object that might be a ship.

The *Suroit* found several such objects. The Americans arrived on August 5, in the *Knorr*, and used *Argo* to check out the sources of the signals. Alas, none was a ship at all, much less the *Titanic*. The search was widened.

For weeks, the *Argo* in tow, the *Knorr* crisscrossed a small portion of ocean, a search technique known as "mowing the grass." Riding along only 75 feet (22.5 m) above the ocean floor, *Argo* broadcast a stream of live television images, which were monitored aboard the *Knorr*. As time passed and no *Titanic* appeared, one can imagine how discouraged the American oceanographers and geologists must have become.

At one o'clock in the morning on September 1, 1985, a large black shape hove into view. Blurry at first, it rapidly became recognizable as the boiler of a very large ship.

The *Titanic!*

In a succession of stunning images, the long-sunken *Titanic* was revealed on the television screen: the crow's nest from which the lookout first saw the approaching iceberg; part of the telephone from which he called his warning to the bridge; the hole left behind when one of the giant smokestacks was ripped loose as the ship sank; bedsprings; chamber pots; and bottles of wine.

The sight was almost too much for the crew of the *Knorr*, who had practically lived with the story of the *Titanic* for months in preparation for its rediscovery. In respect to those who had died aboard the *Titanic*, the crew of the *Knorr* held an impromptu memorial service. As Ballard later described it in an interview pub-

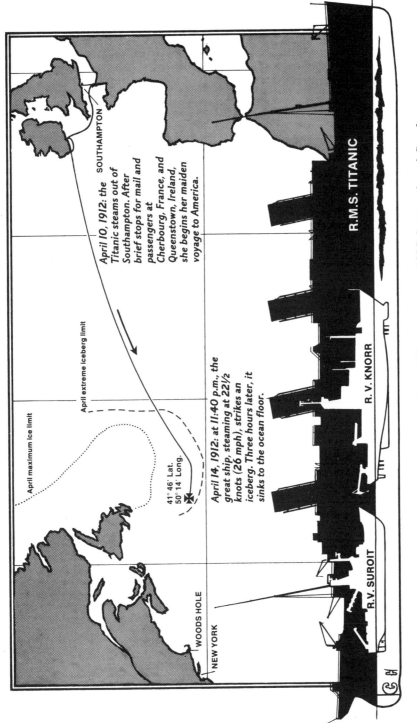

April 10, 1912: the Titanic steams out of Southampton. After brief stops for mail and passengers at Cherbourg, France, and Queenstown, Ireland, she begins her maiden voyage to America.

April extreme iceberg limit

April maximum ice limit

41° 46' Lat.
50° 14' Long.

April 14, 1912: at 11:40 p.m., the great ship, steaming at 22½ knots (26 mph), strikes an iceberg. Three hours later, it sinks to the ocean floor.

SOUTHAMPTON

WOODS HOLE

NEW YORK

R.M.S. TITANIC

R.V. KNORR

R.V. SUROIT

In the joint U. S./French exploration, the French research vessel Suroit prepared the way by narrowing the search area with sonar scanners.

Aboard the research vessel Knorr, scientists from France and Woods Hole Oceanographic Institution located and photographed the doomed liner.

A 300-foot tear through five of her watertight compartments sent the Titanic to her final resting place, more than 12,000 feet down.

Above: *The port side of the bow of the* Titanic. *Two capstans, a port, and a starboard chain can be detected.* Below: *A piece of the ship's ribbing, showing the perfectly polished brass rim of a porthole.*

*One of the davits that secured a lifeboat to the* Titanic *extends over the edge of the hull.*

lished in *Omni* magazine: "I didn't expect the *Titanic* to hit me emotionally. The ship itself had such an impact. I had researched the disaster in intricate detail to find it. And suddenly there it was! . . . There were the empty lifeboat davits hanging there with no boats. To me that was the symbolism of the *Titanic*—the empty lifeboat davits. . . . To come up finally, particularly from the second or third class, to the boat deck and find all the lifeboats gone. Gone!"[12]

Now that the *Titanic* has been found, what will be done with it? Will it be raised, as suggested by one popular novel and movie (*Raise the Titanic!*) of the 1970s? We do not know yet. Ballard believes that the ship should be left precisely where it is, as a memorial both to the victims and survivors of the wreck. For that reason, he will not reveal the precise location where the *Titanic* was found. But there are others who want to see it raised.

If someone wants to raise the *Titanic* or just ransack it for valuables, is there anything to stop them? There may not be, at least legally speaking. No one really owns the *Titanic*, or at least no one has yet come forth with proof of ownership. The Cunard Line, which merged more than fifty years ago with the *Titanic*'s original owner, White Star Lines, claims that the liner is not their property. And for complex legal reasons the insurance company that paid the claim on the ship may no longer retain the rights to it. In addition, the ship lies in international waters. If someone wants to salvage it, the *Titanic* may be fair game. In fact, in the summer of 1987, a French team from IFREMER set out for the site of the *Titanic* with the expressed intention of retrieving valuables from the ship.

Of course, sheer logistics will make all but the rich and powerful—and determined—think twice about raising the ship. The 46,328-ton ship is 2.5 miles (4 km) down in an undersea realm where the water puts 6,000 pounds (2,700 kg) of pressure on every square inch of the ship. Although it has been suggested that the ship be surrounded with inflatable canvas bags and floated to the surface, this would certainly be the most ambitious ship-raising job of all times and may not even be possible using current technology. Oilman Jack Grimm, who does not believe the ship can be raised, plans to use a fleet of midget submarines to search it for valuables, which may or may not be there.

In July 1986, Ballard and his Wood's Hole team made a second trip to the *Titanic* site on board the research ship *Atlantis II*, and this time they took along even more equipment for deep-sea exploration. This included the midget submarine *Alvin* and a much more sophisticated robot than those used previously, called Jason, Jr., which was tethered directly to the *Alvin*. Jason is a kind of floating "eye," capable of making subtle underwater maneuvers and sending back high-resolution color pictures—even in 3-D!

Ballard and two other team members descended in the *Alvin* directly to the deck of the sunken *Titanic*. "It was like landing on

*Jason, Jr., leaves its "garage" aboard
the manned submersible* Alvin *and sets out to
photograph the remains of the* Titanic.

the moon," said Ballard.[13] For the first time, they were actually on board the ship, instead of viewing it via a television camera. It was a stunning moment. They sent Jason down the grand promenade staircase and into the interior of the ship, where it descended four levels deep, passing by deck after deck. Jason was returned to the exterior of the ship only when the team became afraid that it would become entangled in loose wires dangling from the ceiling of the wreck.

The pictures from inside the ship were dazzling. Chandeliers still hung from the ceiling, although exotic sea creatures had taken up residence on them, giving them the look of stalactites hanging from the ceiling of an icy cavern. Another kind of stalactite had also formed, made of long columns of rust hanging down in bright colors. Artifacts such as dishes and wine bottles were spotted. All of the brass portions of the ship looked beautifully polished, although the wood had been largely eaten away by underwater organisms. There was no sign of the ship's passengers or crew.

On the sixth day of this second exploration, the passengers of the *Alvin* found one of the *Titanic*'s large safes lying outside the ship, near the stern. The safes are prime targets of those who wish to salvage the wreckage of the ship. An attempt was made to open the safe, but it was unsuccessful.

Above: *long columns of "rusticles" can be seen covering portholes on the side of the ship photographed by the* Alvin. Below: *cameras reveal a silver serving platter (top center) and some lumps of coal in the debris surrounding the* Titanic.

* * * *

The abilities of tools such as the *Argo* and Jason—and the next generation of minisubmarines and robots that will eventually replace them—are impressive and will extend the abilities of undersea archaeologists into regions where they have so far been unable to go. Do such robots mean that humans have a limited future in undersea research, particularly deep-sea research?

This is a subject of considerable controversy. Science writer Walter Sullivan, in *Oceans* magazine, compares it to the ongoing controversy in the space program over the necessity for sending astronauts into space as opposed to sending unmanned probes.[14]

Ultimately, the answer is probably no. Human beings will not be replaced. Although robots may be built that can explore the sea bottom (or outer space) with as great, or greater, efficiency than a human being, there is something to the human presence that can never be replaced. The ability of a human being to describe a scene that no one has ever witnessed before, and the need for an on-the-spot archaeologist to direct the exploration and study of a site, will always be strong; these tasks can never be fully mechanized. People will always dive into the ocean, whatever the risk. It's part of being an exploring species.

# CHAPTER SEVEN

# RAISING
# THE
# SHUTTLE

What of the undersea archaeologists of the future? Perhaps, with the aid of robots and submersibles that we cannot even imagine today, they will raise from the bottom of the ocean relics of the boats of today . . . or of tomorrow.

For a glimpse at what the undersea archaeology of the future may be like, let's look at the study of two very modern sunken ships, an airship. . . and a spaceship.

**\* \* \* \***

On June 23, 1985, an Air India Boeing 747 en route from Canada to Bombay, India, disappeared from flight controllers' radar screens while flying over the North Atlantic. The suddenness of the disappearance, and the nature of the final messages received from the plane, pointed to the possibility that a terrorist bomb had exploded aboard the plane. In fact, shortly after the incident, two terrorist groups took credit for having blown it up. But terrorist groups are well known for their willingness to take credit for any kind of nefarious act, whether they have actually committed it or not.

It was obvious that uncovering the truth would be difficult at best, because the airplane had gone down in water more than a mile (1.6 km) deep. The parts of the airplane that most interested investigators were the so-called "black boxes," recording devices (not actually black in color) that keep records of the airplane's position, speed, and other vital statistics, as well as recordings of all conversations in the cockpit. But how to get to the black boxes that lay at the bottom of the ocean?

The answer was to use *SCARAB I* and *SCARAB II*, remote-controlled minisub devices developed by AT&T for repairing underwater telephone cables. The *SCARAB*s—the name stands for *s*ubmersible *c*raft for *a*ssisting *r*epair *a*nd *b*urial—were designed for working in depths just about as great as the depth of the Air India wreckage; they work at the end of a 10,000-foot (3,000-m) cable that keeps them in contact with the "mother ship."

Unlike *Argo*, the *SCARAB*s can do more than just look around underwater. They possess "claws" that can manipulate and pick up objects. The *SCARAB*s can lift objects weighing up to 500 pounds (225 kg) and bring them to the surface, provided they can get a good "grip."

And the *SCARAB*s proved as good as their reputation by retrieving the black boxes from the wreckage. Alas, the tapes were inconclusive. Apparently, the black boxes had stopped operating shortly before the crash. The investigators returned to the spot to use the *SCARAB*s, along with a special lifting cable device called a ram tensioner, to retrieve more pieces of the wreckage along with the bodies of passengers.

As the pieces were raised, however, the mystery deepened. There was no direct evidence of an explosion, but there was an indication that passengers in the rear of the plane had been subject to some kind of sudden trauma, possibly caused by an explosion in the baggage compartment below them.

The implications for undersea archaeologists in the use of tools like the *SCARAB*s are obvious, and the notion of using such tools

*SCARAB, a remote-controlled minisub
developed by AT&T, could be extremely
useful for future underwater research.*

to investigate a modern airship like a Boeing 747 gives us a glimpse of what the archaeologist of the future may be studying beneath the waves.

\* \* \* \*

On January 28, 1986, while millions of schoolchildren and others watched on TVs around the United States, the space shuttle *Challenger* roared off its launch pad in Cape Canaveral, Florida. Aboard was a crew of seven, including astronauts, mission specialists, and a teacher. Slightly more than a minute into the mission, the shuttle exploded in a plume of white smoke seen on television screens all over the world.

For what seemed like hours afterward (but was actually a little more than nine minutes), the many pieces of the shuttle drifted back to earth, some of them tumbling quickly, some of them floating down more leisurely. The pieces landed in the waters of the Atlantic Ocean and, in many cases, sank to the bottom. To find out exactly what had happened to the *Challenger*, investigators needed to raise the remains of this futuristic spaceship from the bottom of the ocean, just as undersea archaeologists had raised more traditional ships, such as the *Vasa*, from their watery graves. The search for the shuttle turned out to be what *The Washington Post* has described as "the largest underwater search and salvage operation in history."[15]

*The space shuttle* Challenger *is seen here lifting off in a successful mission in February 1984. In January 1986, it exploded in a plume of white smoke, killing the entire crew and destroying the craft.*

The operation involved not only the National Aeronautics and Space Administration (NASA), but the U.S. Navy, Air Force, and Coast Guard, as well as private salvage contractors. In addition to an oil ship with a lifting crane, a pair of miniature submarines called Johnson Sea-Link subs, and various ships and aircraft, the search party had the full-time use of the world's smallest nuclear submarine!

* * * *

The search covered a vast area. Four ships equipped with sonar crisscrossed the water on parallel courses, recording (by the end of the search) more than 5,000 miles (8,000 km) worth of sonar images. These images were examined by a sonar expert for signs of underwater objects that might be pieces of the shuttle.

The major object of the search was the *Challenger*'s right solid rocket booster, or SRB, which was later identified as the cause of the explosion. Complicating the sonar search for the booster was the fact that the waters where the shuttle debris landed were already filled with junk, including (as the searchers eventually discovered) a Pershing missile, a sunken freighter, and a DC-3 airplane left over from World War II.

When a likely looking blip appeared on the sonar record, a submarine was dispatched to take a closer look. The nuclear submarine, called the *NR1*, checked out most of the sonar signals. It could stay underwater for days at a time. The minisubs also checked out several sonar contacts (as they were called) per day.

Over the course of the operation, 722 sonar contacts were singled out as being worth a closer look. The one that finally paid off was contact 131. The *NR1* nuclear sub dived within 20 feet (6 m) of it, took a few photographs, and passed the photos on to NASA. It was partially buried, and not immediately recognizable as an important piece of wreckage, but NASA investigators thought that they saw signs that the object, whatever it was, had been badly burned, as the SRB would have been during the explosion of the

*This piece of the debris from*
*Challenger's right wing was recovered*
*during the extensive salvage operation.*

shuttle. So one of the Johnson Sea-Link minisubs was sent to check it out a second time, on April 11.

After a lengthy investigation of the site, the two men in the minisub attached cables to the piece of debris and towed it back to the oil ship, called the *Stena Workhorse*. The oil ship crane was lowered into the water and attached to the debris. When it was lifted onto the deck of the ship, its identity became obvious. It was the *Challenger*'s right SRB, and it was burned in exactly the way the investigators had believed it would be. It was the final evidence that NASA had needed to prove that the SRB had been responsible for the explosion.

# CHAPTER EIGHT

# THE HUMAN ELEMENT

Undersea archaeology is an exciting field with an exciting future. As we said in the first chapter, one of the great advantages of this area of archaeological research is that artifacts may remain unmolested beneath the ocean for thousands of years.

Yet, in some ways, that may no longer be true.

Cousteau's scuba gear opened a new age for the undersea archaeologist, but it also opened a new frontier for the average person. Almost anyone can afford to buy or rent the gear necessary to explore the relatively shallow waters where many wrecks are found. With no knowledge of archaeology at all, these treasure hunters can examine wrecks and even bring up artifacts of their own, depriving the archaeologist and historian of these finds and even destroying the information contained in the wreck that is left behind.

And not all of the treasure hunters are amateurs. Some of them are professionals, with sophisticated equipment at their command. They sell the contents of old ships to anyone who is interested in such things and can afford the cost.

To archaeologists, this is heresy. As undersea archaeologist George Fisher puts it: "The first commandment is: Thou shalt not sell the goodies!"[16]

The goodies, in this case, are objects of historical value, which the archaeologist holds as sacrosanct. The treasure hunter usually has fewer qualms. An important issue, however, is that of ownership. Who do materials found at the bottom of the sea belong to? Ancient maritime law gives the salvager the rights to abandoned shipwrecks in international waters, but much of the material under contention lies in the shallow waters off of sovereign territory, and this makes the ownership issue trickier. Such questions are even now being thrashed out in the courts. And, in many instances, the courts are finding in favor of the treasure hunters. At least one bill has been put before Congress to give the federal government ownership of sunken ships found on the so-called outer continental shelf, but this legislation has yet to pass.

\* \* \* \*

Does this mean that the future of undersea archaeology is somehow in doubt? Hardly. Even if much of the history that lies under the water is plundered by those who prefer quick money to preserving history, there will be artifacts available to the archaeologist for a long time to come.

The sea is a giant museum, and there is a little something in it for everyone to look at, amateur and archaeologist alike. It will be a long time before the sea divulges all of its mysteries. Unlike Mussolini and his lake, we will probably never be able to drain the oceans and pick the interesting materials off the bottom. Centuries from now new treasures, in both the historical and monetary sense, will still be rising from the deep, discovered by increasingly sophisticated instruments that will plunge into the deepest of ocean depths and unearth the human past, in a realm where once only the fish dwelt.

# NOTES

1. Peter Throckmorton, *Shipwrecks and Archaeology: The Unharvested Sea* (Boston: Little, Brown, 1970).
2. *Ibid.*
3. Jacques Cousteau, *The Silent World* (New York: Harper & Row, 1953).
4. Jacques Cousteau, *The Living Sea* (New York: Ballantine, 1975), 48.
5. *Ibid.,* 53.
6. A. Morland, "Back from the Deep: Restoration of the *Vasa,*" *Oceans*, March–April 1985, 16.
7. *Ibid.*
8. G. Russell, "Raising a Tudor *Rose*," *Time*, 25 October 1982, 89.
9. *Ibid.*
10. Margaret Rule, "Henry VIII's Lost Warship," *National Geographic*, May 1983, 646.
11. *Ibid.,* 652.
12. Quote by D. Colligan, *Omni*, July 1986, 60.
13. Quoted in *The Washington Post*, 31 July 1986, 1.

14. Walter Sullivan, "Deep Seeing," *Oceans*, Jan.–Feb. 1986, 18.
15. Quoted in *The Washington Post*, 28 May 1986, 1.
16. Philip Trupp, "Ancient Shipwrecks Yield Both Prizes and Bitter Controversy," *Smithsonian*, October 1983, 78.

# GLOSSARY

**amphora**—a vase-like container used for packing and storage by the ancient Greeks; the plural is *amphorae.*

**archaeologist**—a historian-scientist who studies artifacts from the past.

**artifact**—a manufactured object, such as a pot or a statue, as opposed to something that occurs naturally, such as a rock or a living creature.

**bends**—a deadly and painful condition in which nitrogen bubbles build up in the bloodstream of a diver who surfaces too quickly from a deep dive.

**coring device**—a tube used to bring up samples of sediment from the ocean floor.

**diving bells**—bell-shaped chambers in which human beings can descend beneath the water without wearing diving suits or scuba gear.

**diving flippers**—web-footed contraptions worn on the feet to aid a diver in moving forward through the water.

**diving mask**—a glass-plated device that straps to the face of a diver to improve vision underwater.

**nitrogen narcosis**—a deadly, if pleasurable, condition in which a buildup of nitrogen in the blood causes a diver to become giddy and almost drunken; also called *rapture of the depths.*

**recompression chamber**—enclosed chamber that simulates the high air pressures experienced by divers; used for curing the bends.

**scuba**—*s*elf-*c*ontained *u*nderwater *b*reathing *a*pparatus; a combination of air tanks, rubber hoses, and a breathing valve that allows a diver to carry a supply of air on a long dive.

**snorkel**—a rubber tube through which a diver just below the surface of the water can breathe.

**sonar**—a device that uses sound waves and their echoes to detect solid objects underwater; short for *so*und *na*vigation and *r*anging.

**submarine archaeology**—see *undersea archaeology.*

**teredo**—an underwater worm that eats the wood from wrecked ships; also called a *shipworm.*

**undersea archaeology**—the study of artifacts found beneath the water in an ocean, sea, lake, etc. Also called *underwater* or *submarine archaeology.*

Bass, George. *Archaeology Under Water.* New York: Praeger, 1966. A detailed look at the science of undersea archaeology by one of its foremost practitioners.

Cousteau, Jacques. *The Silent World.* New York: Harper & Row, 1953.

—————————. *The Living Sea.* New York: Harper & Row, 1963. This and the book above are the first two volumes of a fascinating autobiography by the man who revolutionized both diving and underwater archaeology.

Lord, Walter. *A Night to Remember.* New York: Holt, Rinehart & Winston, 1955.

—————————. *The Night Lives On.* New York: Morrow & Co., 1986. This book and the one above are immensely readable accounts of the sinking of the *Titanic.*

McKee, Alexander. *History Under the Sea.* New York: Dutton & Co., 1968. An entertaining history of the field by the man who raised the *Mary Rose.*

Silverberg, Robert. *Sunken History: The Story of Underwater Archaeology.* Philadelphia: Chilton, 1963. A readable account of the early history of undersea archaeology by a noted science fiction writer.

# INDEX